AC/DC

for ukulele

**Twenty-two classic AC/DC rockers arranged for ukulele!
Complete with full lyrics, chord boxes, and all your favorite high-voltage riffs in tablature!**

Music Sales America

DISTRIBUTED BY

HAL•LEONARD®
CORPORATION

7777 W. BLUEMOUND RD. P.O. BOX 13819 MILWAUKEE, WI 53213

Cover photo: David Atlas/Retna Ltd.
Project editor: David Bradley

This book Copyright © 2010 Leidseplein Presse B.V.
Administered by J. Albert & Son Pty Limited

This book published 2010 by Amsco Publications,
A Division of Music Sales Corporation, New York

Order No. AM1000461
International Standard Book Number: 978-0-8256-3742-1
HL Item Number: 14037643

BACK IN BLACK
By Angus Young and Malcolm Young and Brian Johnson

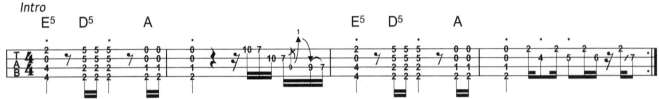

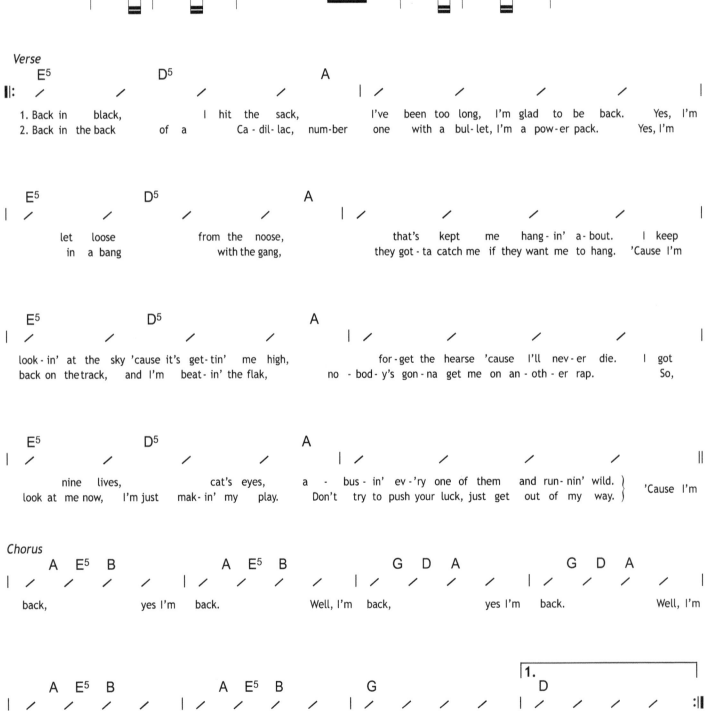

Intro

Verse

1. Back in black, I hit the sack, I've been too long, I'm glad to be back. Yes, I'm
2. Back in the back of a Ca-dil-lac, num-ber one with a bul-let, I'm a pow-er pack. Yes, I'm

let loose from the noose, that's kept me hang-in' a-bout. I keep
in a bang with the gang, they got-ta catch me if they want me to hang. 'Cause I'm

look-in' at the sky 'cause it's get-tin' me high, for-get the hearse 'cause I'll nev-er die. I got
back on the track, and I'm beat-in' the flak, no-bod-y's gon-na get me on an-oth-er rap. So,

nine lives, cat's eyes, a-bus-in' ev-'ry one of them and run-nin' wild. }
look at me now, I'm just mak-in' my play. Don't try to push your luck, just get out of my way. } 'Cause I'm

Chorus

back, yes I'm back. Well, I'm back, yes I'm back. Well, I'm

1.

back, back. Well, I'm back, yes I'm back in black.

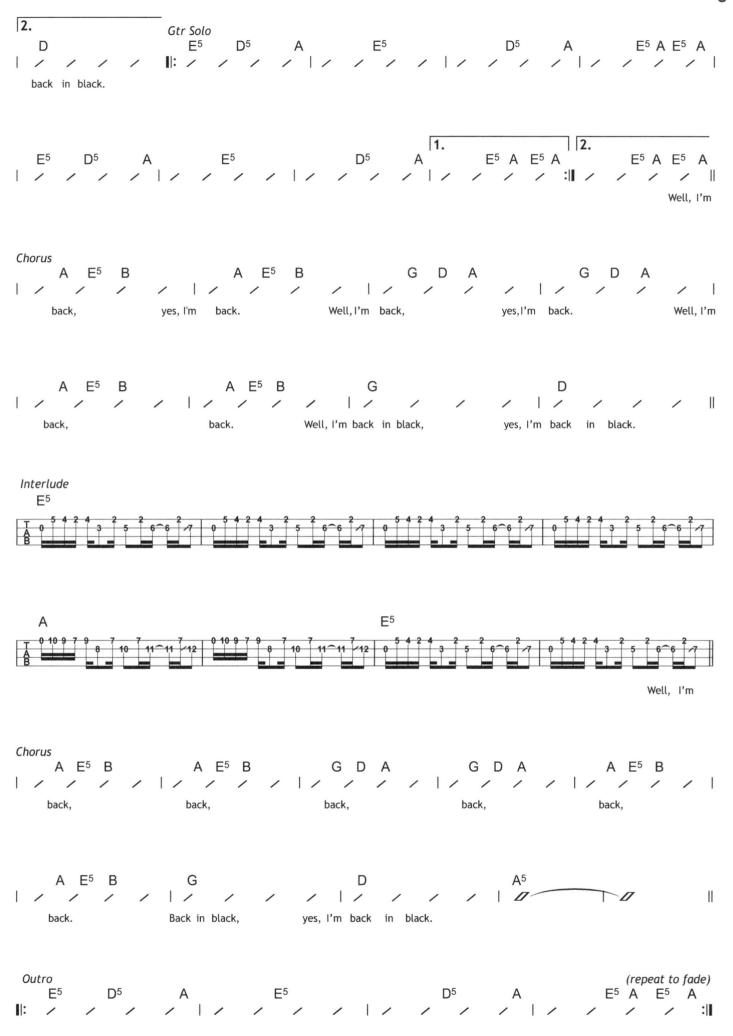

BIG BALLS

By Angus Young, Malcolm Young and Bon Scott

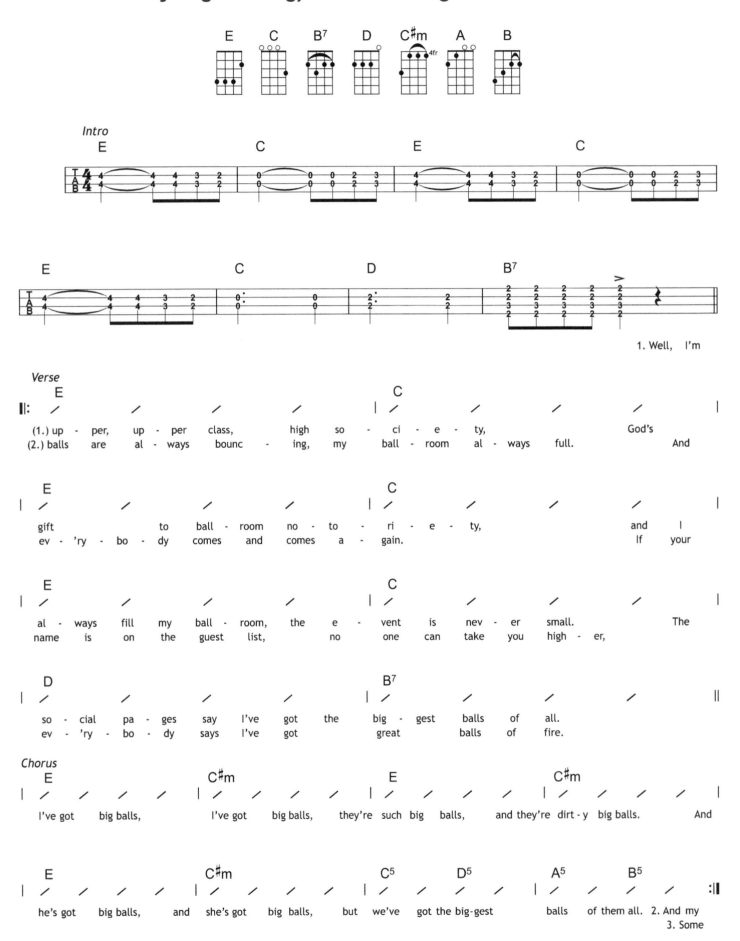

Verse

E				C			

(3.) balls are held for char - i - ty, and some for fan - cy dress, but when

E				C			

they're held for pleas - ure, they're the balls that I like best. My

E				C			

balls are al - ways bounc - ing, to the left and to the right. It's

D				B⁷			

my be - lief that my big balls should be held ev - 'ry night.

Chorus

E		C♯m		E		C♯m	

We've got big balls, we've got big balls, we've got big balls, dirt - y big balls.
And I'm just itch- ing to tell you a-bout them, oh, we have such won-der-ful fun.

E		C♯m		C⁵	D⁵	A⁵	B⁵

He's got big balls, she's got big balls, but we've got the big-gest balls of them all.
Sea - food cock - tail, crabs, cray - fish.

Outro

E				C♯m			

Bol - locks, knack - ers, bol - locks, knack - ers, Bol - locks, knack - ers, bol - locks, knack - ers,

E				C♯m			

Bol - locks, knack - ers, bol - locks, knack - ers, Bol - locks, knack - ers, bol - locks, knack - ers,

E							

Bol - locks, knack - ers, bol - locks, knack - ers, bol - locks.

DIRTY DEEDS DONE DIRT CHEAP

By Angus Young, Malcolm Young and Bon Scott

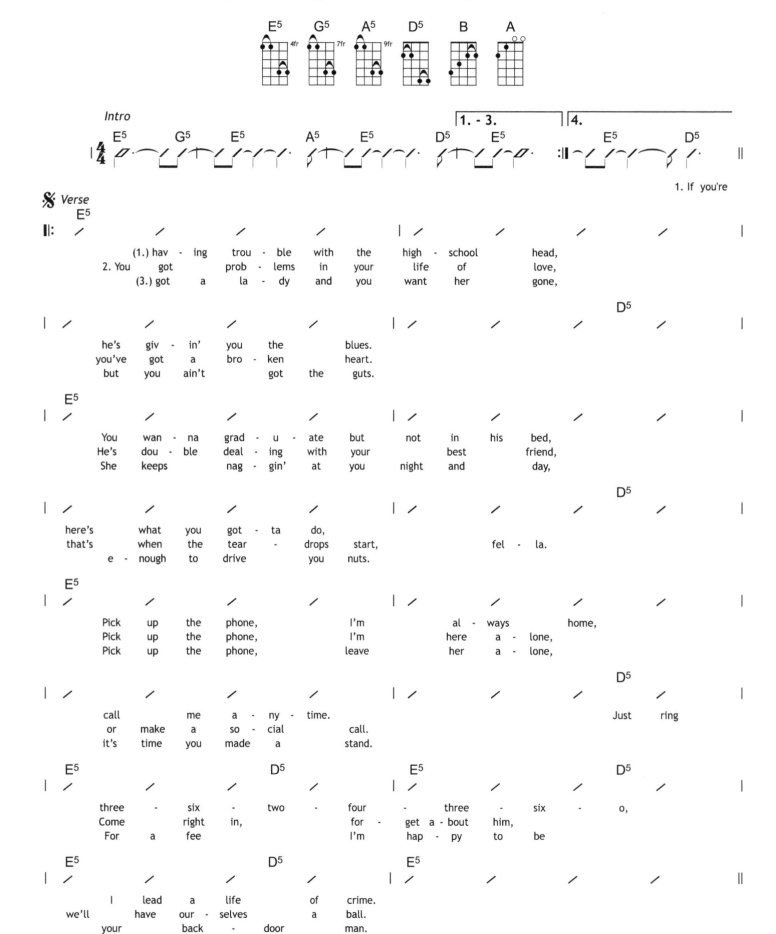

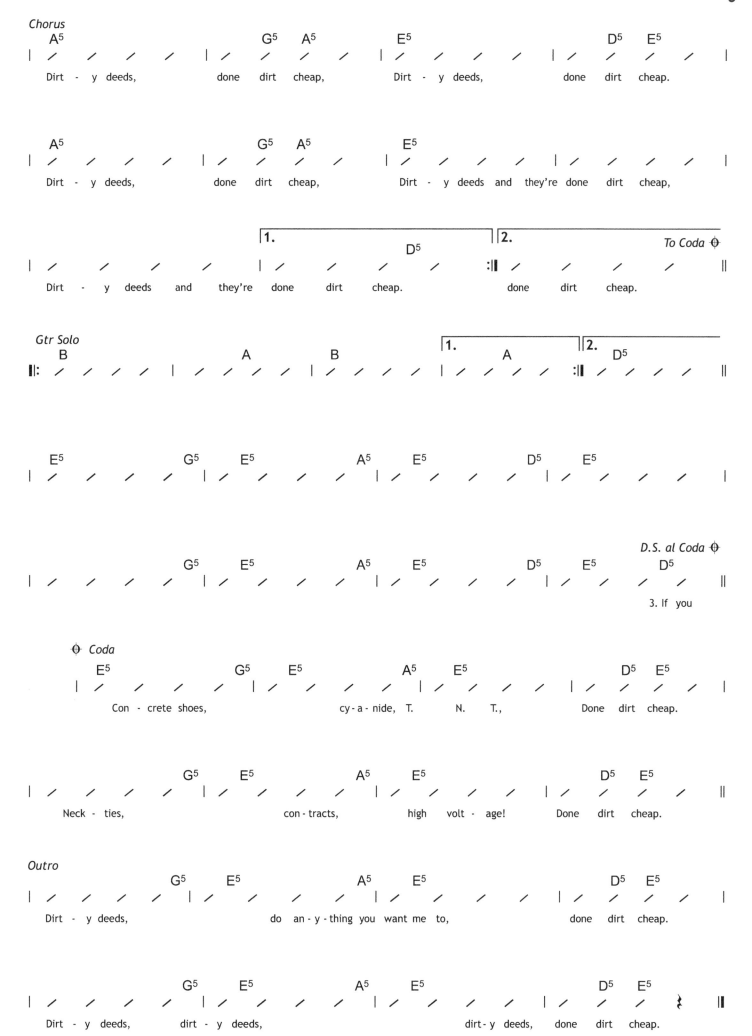

FOR THOSE ABOUT TO ROCK
(WE SALUTE YOU)

By Angus Young and Malcolm Young and Brian Johnson

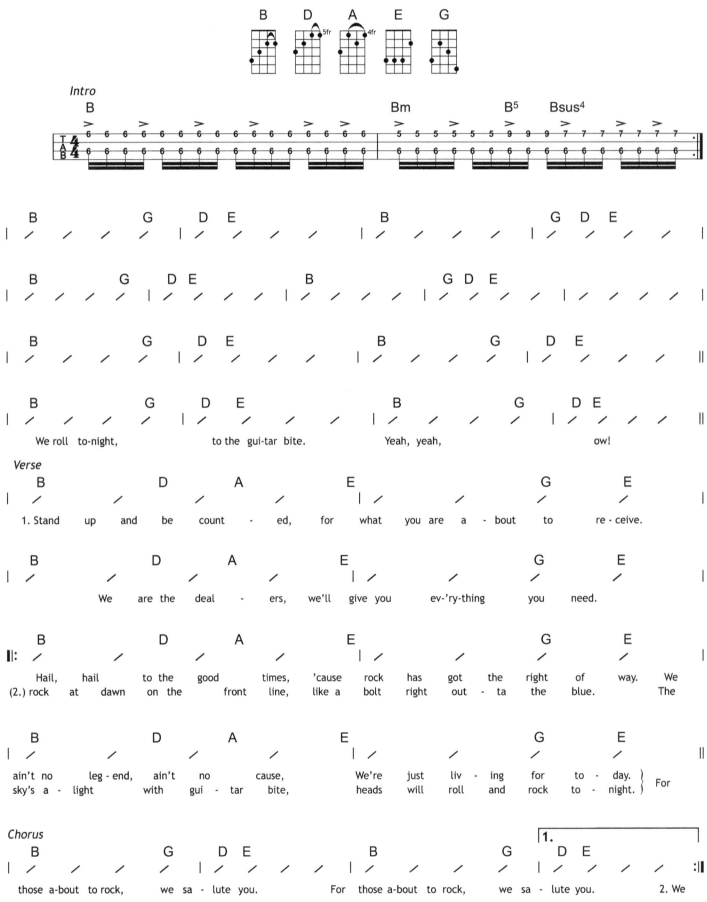

We roll to-night, to the gui-tar bite. Yeah, yeah, ow!

Verse

1. Stand up and be count - ed, for what you are a - bout to re - ceive.

We are the deal - ers, we'll give you ev-'ry-thing you need.

Hail, hail to the good times, 'cause rock has got the right of way. We
(2.) rock at dawn on the front line, like a bolt right out - ta the blue. The

ain't no leg - end, ain't no cause, We're just liv - ing for to - day.
sky's a - light with gui - tar bite, heads will roll and rock to - night. } For

Chorus

those a-bout to rock, we sa - lute you. For those a-bout to rock, we sa - lute you. 2. We

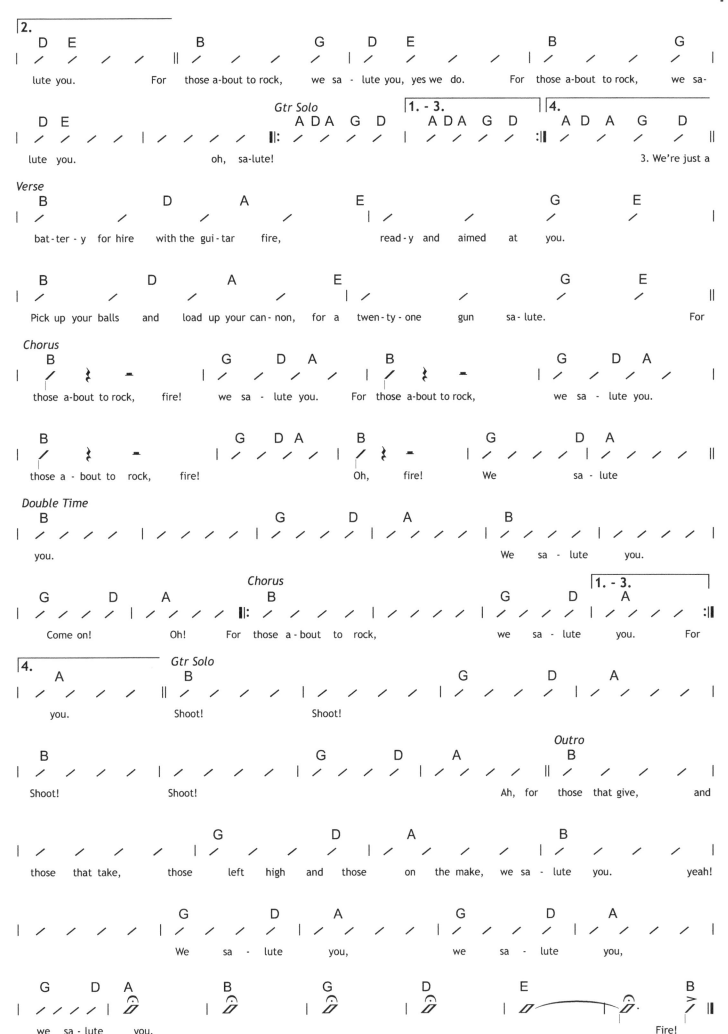

GIRLS GOT RHYTHM

By Angus Young, Malcolm Young and Bon Scott

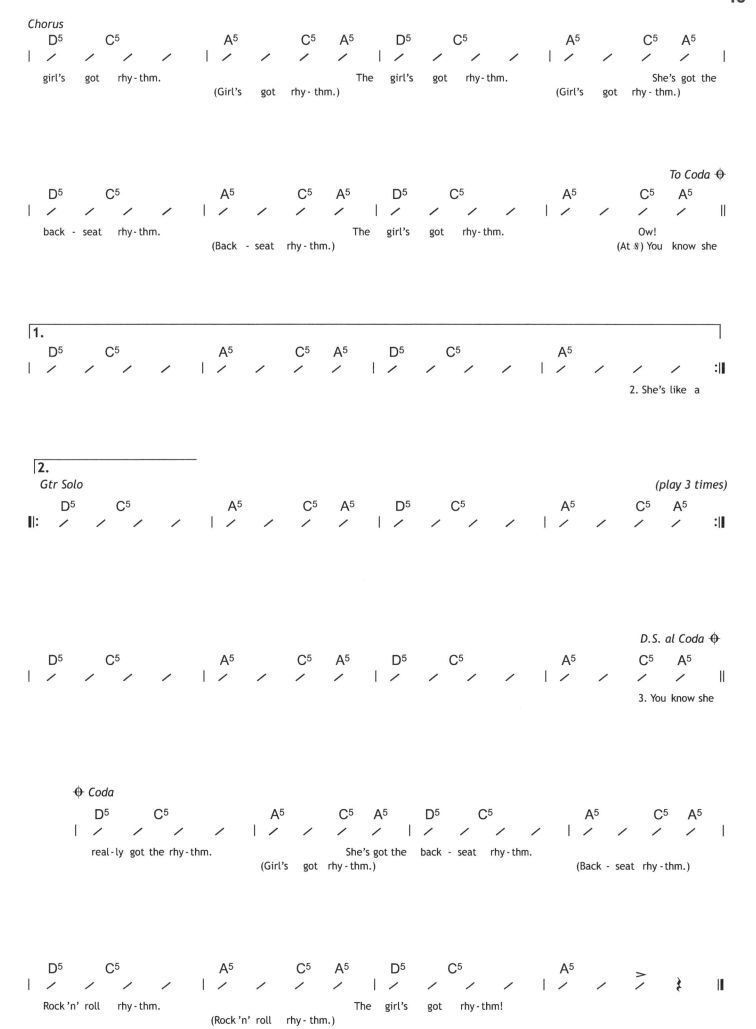

HAVE A DRINK ON ME
By Angus Young and Malcolm Young and Brian Johnson

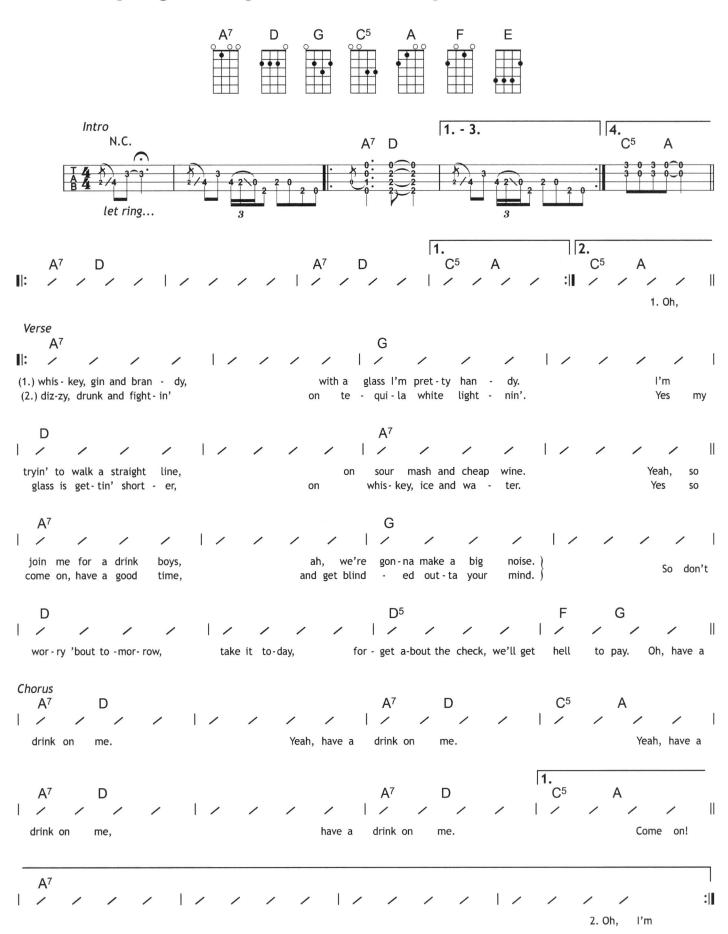

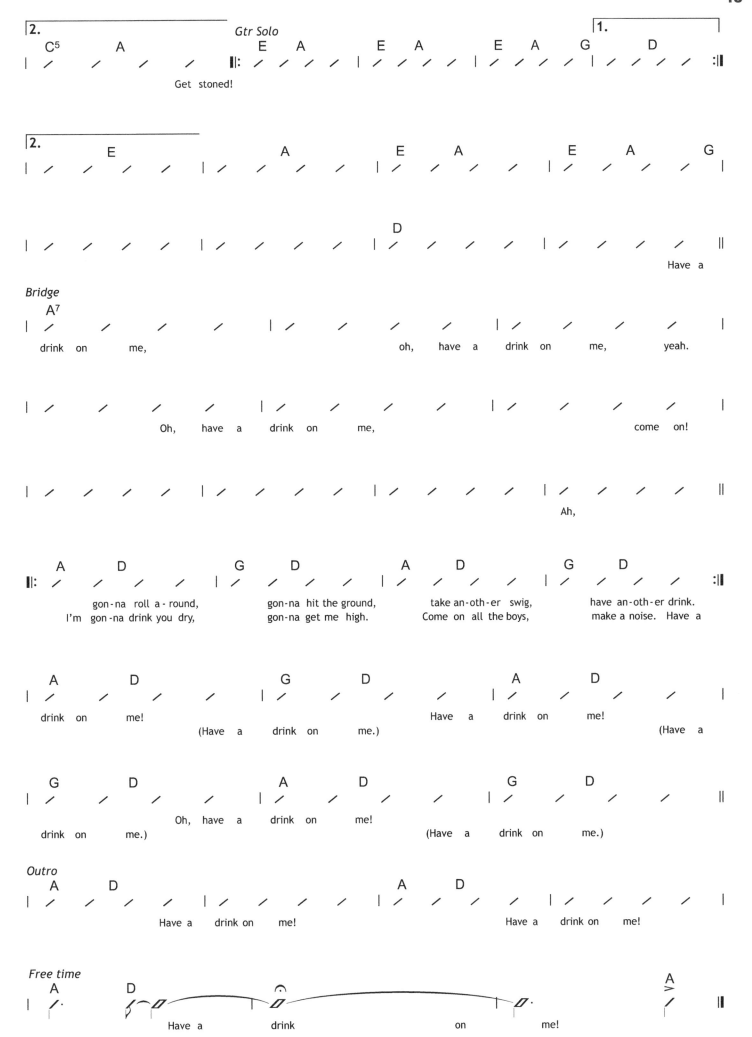

HELLS BELLS
By Angus Young and Malcolm Young and Brian Johnson

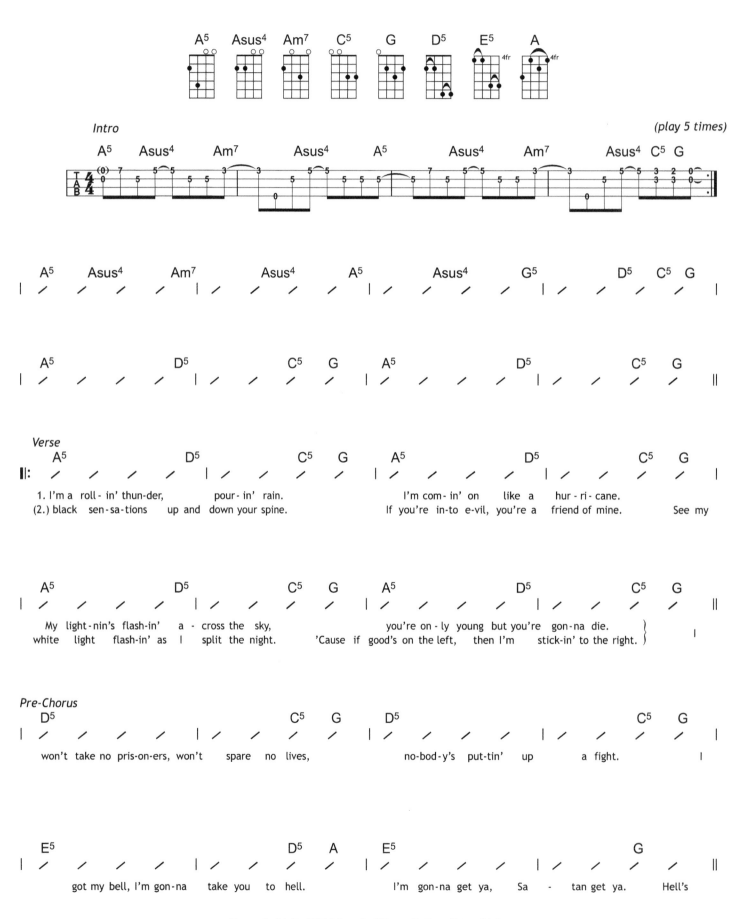

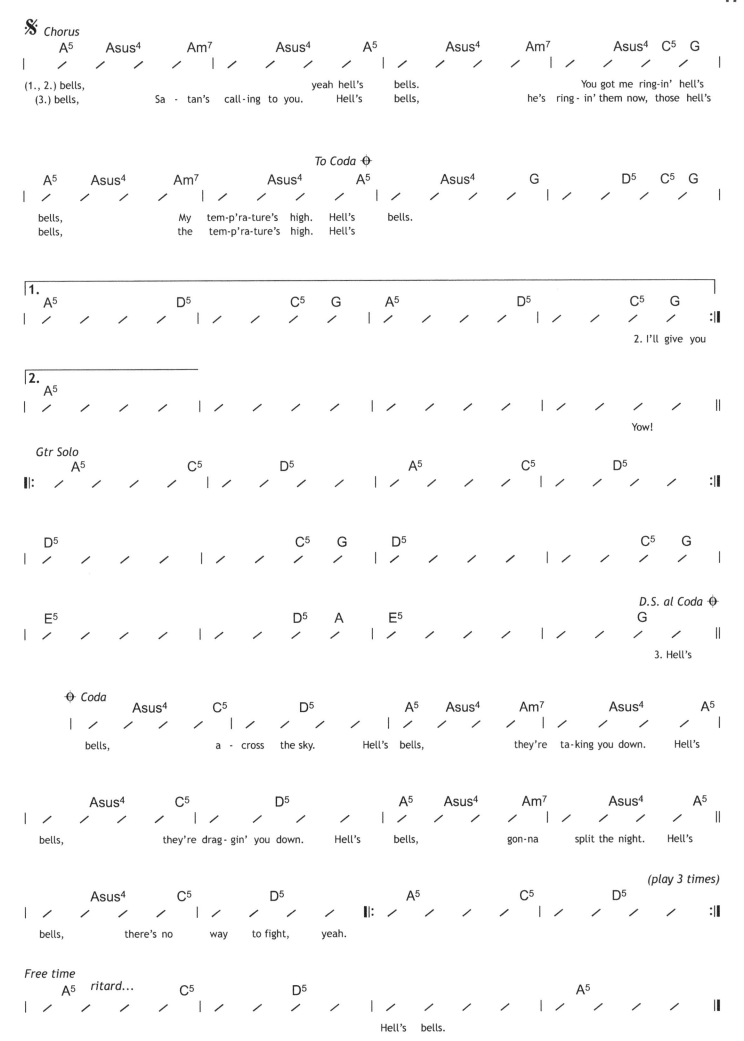

HIGHWAY TO HELL

By Angus Young, Malcolm Young and Bon Scott

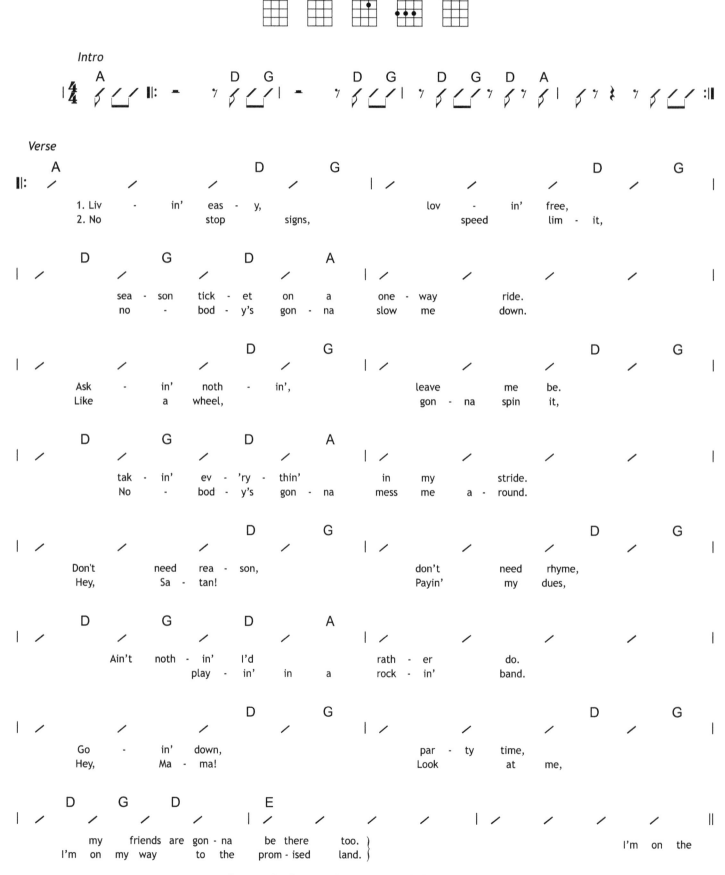

Chorus

A · · · · D · · · · G D A · · · · D · · · · G D

high - way to hell, on the high - way to hell,

A · · · · D · · · · G D A · · · · D **1.** A⁵

high - way to hell, I'm on the high - way to hell.

2. · · · · · G D · · · · G D G D

Mm, don't stop me. Yeah, yeah, ow!

Gtr Solo

A · · · · D · · · · G D A · · · · D · · · · G D

A · · · · D · · · · G D A · · · · D · · · · G D

I'm on the

Chorus

A · · · · D · · · · G D A · · · · D · · · · G D

high - way to hell, on the high - way to hell, I'm on the

A · · · · D · · · · G D A · · · · D · · · · G D

high - way to hell, on the high - way to hell.

Chorus

A · · · · D · · · G D A · · · · D

High - way to hell. High - way to hell.

G D A · · · · D · · · · G D

High - way to hell.

A · · · · D *Free time*

High - way to hell. And I'm go - in' down, all the way. Whoa!

A · A⁶ A

We're on the high - way to hell.

IF YOU WANT BLOOD (YOU'VE GOT IT)

By Angus Young, Malcolm Young and Bon Scott

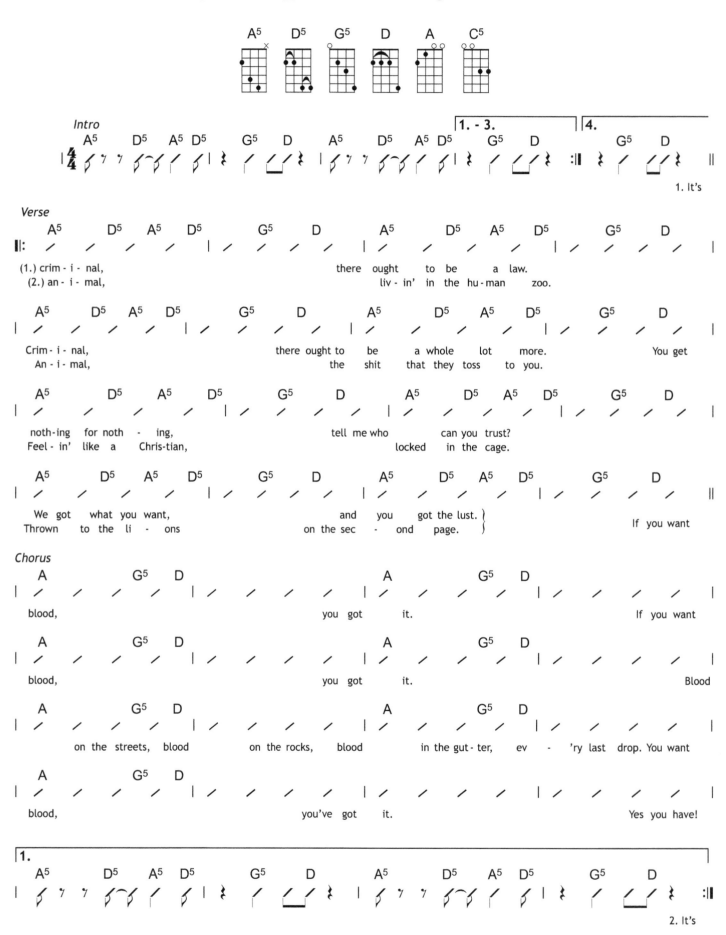

2. ————————————————————————————— *Gtr Solo*   *(play 8 times)*

| / / / / / | / / / / | ‖: A5 D5 A5 D5 G5 D :‖

Oh,   I'm talk - in' to   you!

Interlude

‖: A5 D5 A5 D5 G5 D | A5 D5 A5 D G5 C5 :‖

Bridge

A5 D5 A5 D5 G5 D | A5 D5 A5 D G5 C5 |

Blood   on the rocks,   Blood   on the streets,

A5 D5 A5 D5 G5 D | A5 D5 A5 D G5 C5 |

Blood   in the sky,   Blood   on the seas.   If you want

A   G5 D

blood,   you   got   it.

A5 D5 A5 D5 G5 D | A5 D5 A5 D5 G5 D |

Want you to bleed   for me.

A5 D5 A5 D5 G5 D | A5 D5 A5 D5 G5 D |

If you want

(repeat to fade)

‖: A5 D5 A5 D5 G5 D :‖

blood,   you got   it.   If you want

LET ME PUT MY LOVE INTO YOU
By Angus Young and Malcolm Young and Brian Johnson

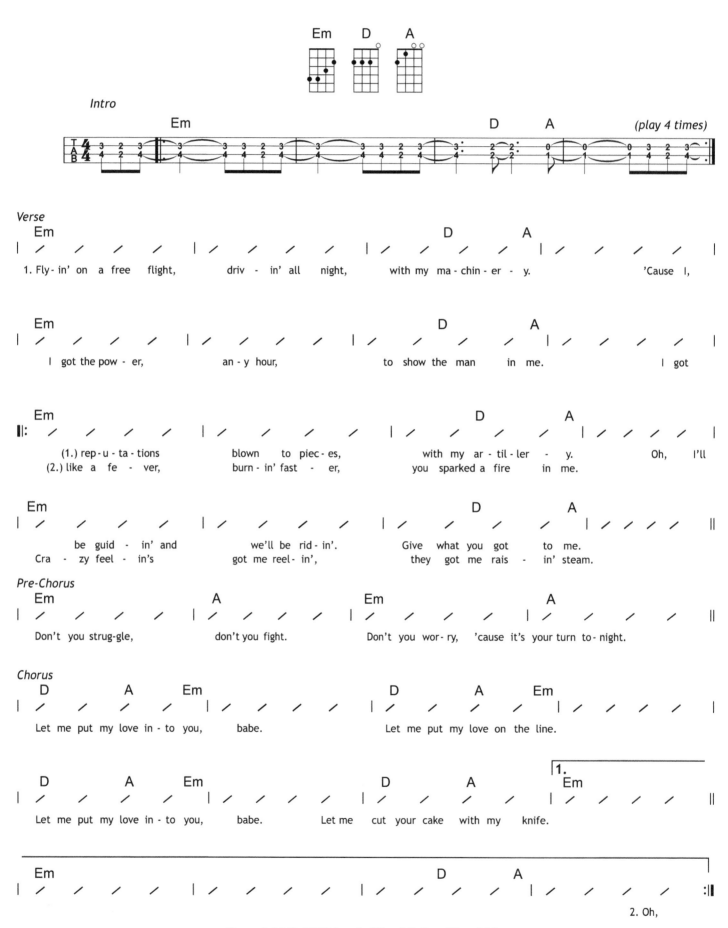

Intro

Em D A

(play 4 times)

Verse

Em   D   A

1. Fly-in' on a free flight, driv-in' all night, with my ma-chin-er-y. 'Cause I,

Em   D   A

I got the pow - er, an - y hour, to show the man in me. I got

Em   D   A

(1.) rep-u-ta-tions blown to piec-es, with my ar-til-ler-y. Oh, I'll

(2.) like a fe-ver, burn-in' fast-er, you sparked a fire in me.

Em   D   A

be guid-in' and we'll be rid-in'. Give what you got to me.

Cra-zy feel-in's got me reel-in', they got me rais-in' steam.

Pre-Chorus

Em   A   Em   A

Don't you strug-gle, don't you fight. Don't you wor-ry, 'cause it's your turn to-night.

Chorus

D   A   Em   D   A   Em

Let me put my love in - to you, babe. Let me put my love on the line.

1.

D   A   Em   D   A   Em

Let me put my love in - to you, babe. Let me cut your cake with my knife.

Em   D   A

2. Oh,

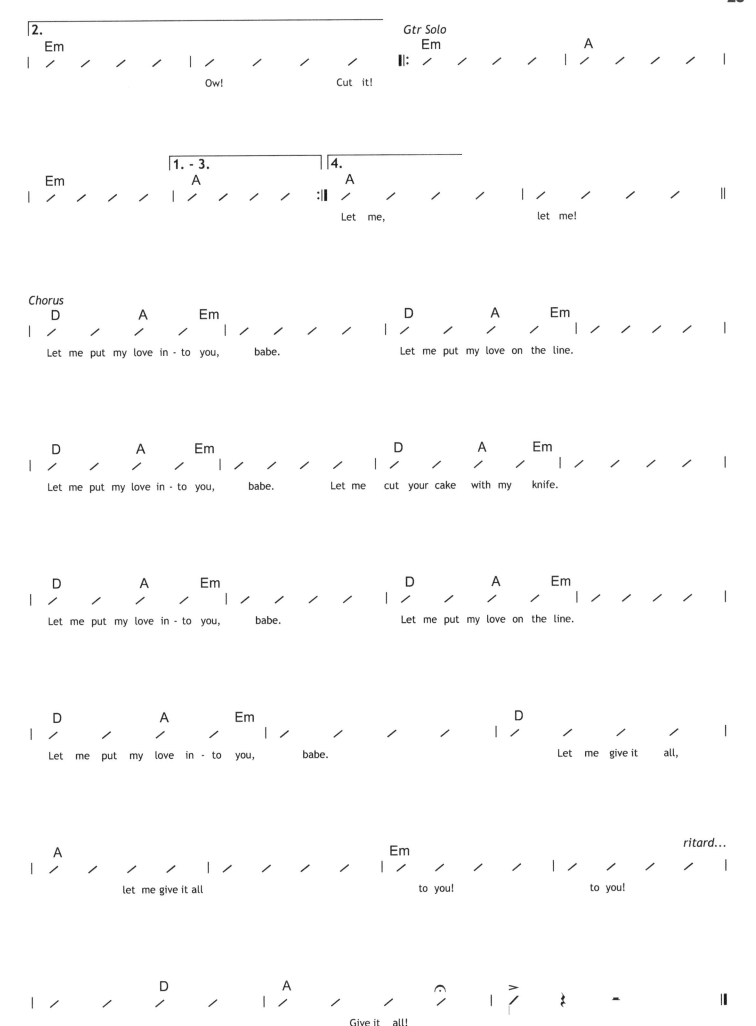

MONEYTALKS

By Angus Young and Malcolm Young

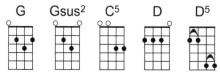

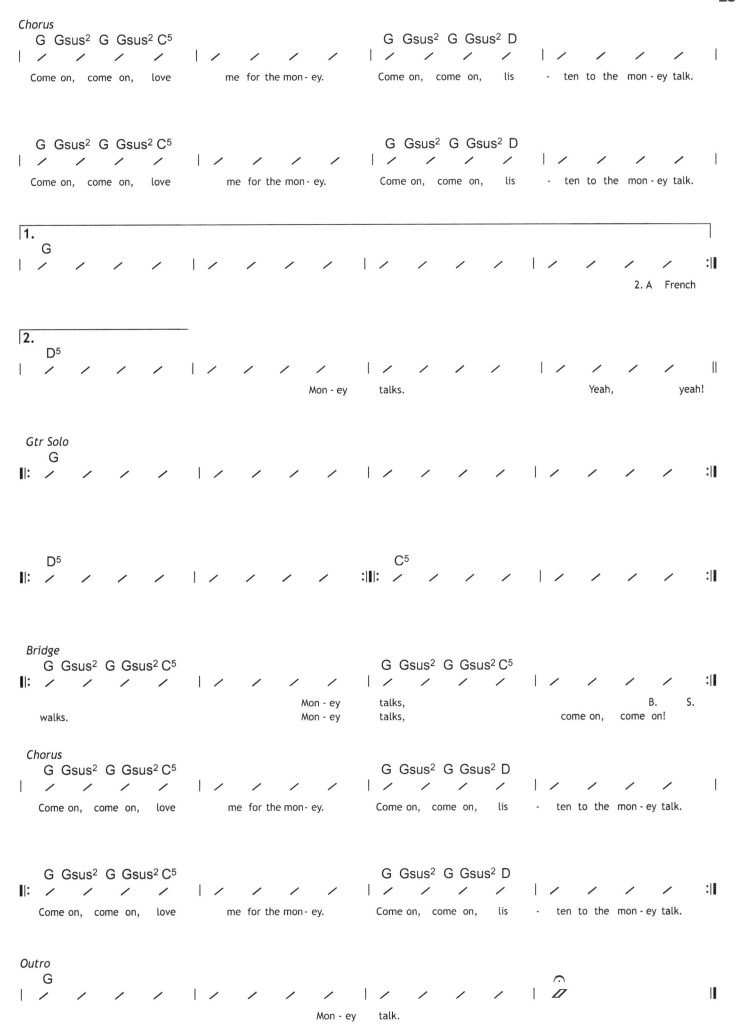

PROBLEM CHILD

By Angus Young, Malcolm Young and Bon Scott

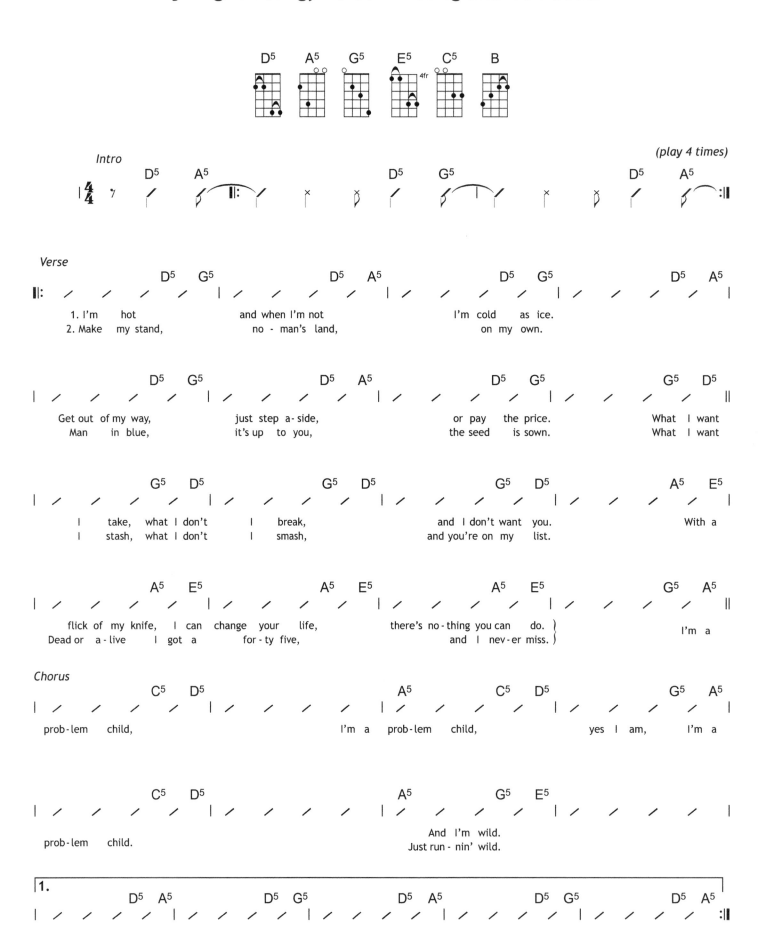

2. ———————— *Gtr Solo*

| / / / / ‖: / / / / | / / / / :‖‖: / / / / | / / / / :‖
       B   D⁵ E⁵   *(play 4 times)*   A⁵   C⁵ D⁵   *(play 3 times)*

A⁵   G⁵ E⁵

| / / / / | / / / / | / / / / | / / / / | / / / / | / / / / ‖
                                            D⁵ A⁵

1. **2.**

‖: / / / / | / / / / | / / / / | / / / / :‖ / / / / ‖
D⁵ G⁵   D⁵ A⁵   D⁵ G⁵   D⁵ A⁵   D⁵ A⁵

Verse

D⁵ G⁵   D⁵ A⁵   D⁵ G⁵   D⁵ A⁵

3. Ev - 'ry night,   street a - light,   I drink my booze.

D⁵ G⁵   D⁵ A⁵   D⁵ G⁵   G⁵ D⁵

Some run,   some fight,   but I win, they lose.   What I need

G⁵ D⁵   G⁵ D⁵   G⁵ D⁵   A⁵ E⁵

I like, what I don't   I fight,   and I don't like you.

A⁵ E⁵   A⁵ E⁵   A⁵ E⁵   G⁵ A⁵

Say bye - bye while you're still a - live,   you're time is through.   'Cause I'm a

Chorus

C⁵ D⁵   A⁵   C⁵ D⁵   G⁵ A⁵

prob-lem child,   I'm a prob-lem child,   I'm a

1.

C⁵ D⁵   A⁵   C⁵ D⁵   G⁵ A⁵

prob-lem child,   I'm a prob-lem child,

2. ———————— *Gtr Solo*

A⁵ B   D⁵ E⁵   A⁵ B

Prob - lem child.

(play 11 times)   *(play 5 times)* ⌒

D⁵ E⁵   A⁵ B   B

Prob - lem child.

ROCK AND ROLL AIN'T NOISE POLLUTION

By Angus Young, Malcolm Young and Brian Johnson

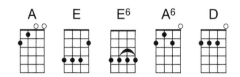

Alright. Hey there all you middle men, throw away your fancy clothes. And while you're out there sittin' on a fence, so get off your ass and come down here, 'cause rock 'n' roll ain't no riddle, man. To me, it makes good, good sense.

Verse

1. Heav - y de - ci - bels are play - in' on my gui - tar, we got vi -
2. I took a look in - side your bed - room door, you

bra - tions com - in' up from the floor. Well, just list -
looked so good ly - in' on your bed. Well, I asked

- 'nin' to the rock that's giv - in' too much noise, are you
you if you want - ed an - y rhy - thm in love, you said you

deaf, you wan - na hear some more? }
wan - na rock 'n' roll in - stead. }

We're just

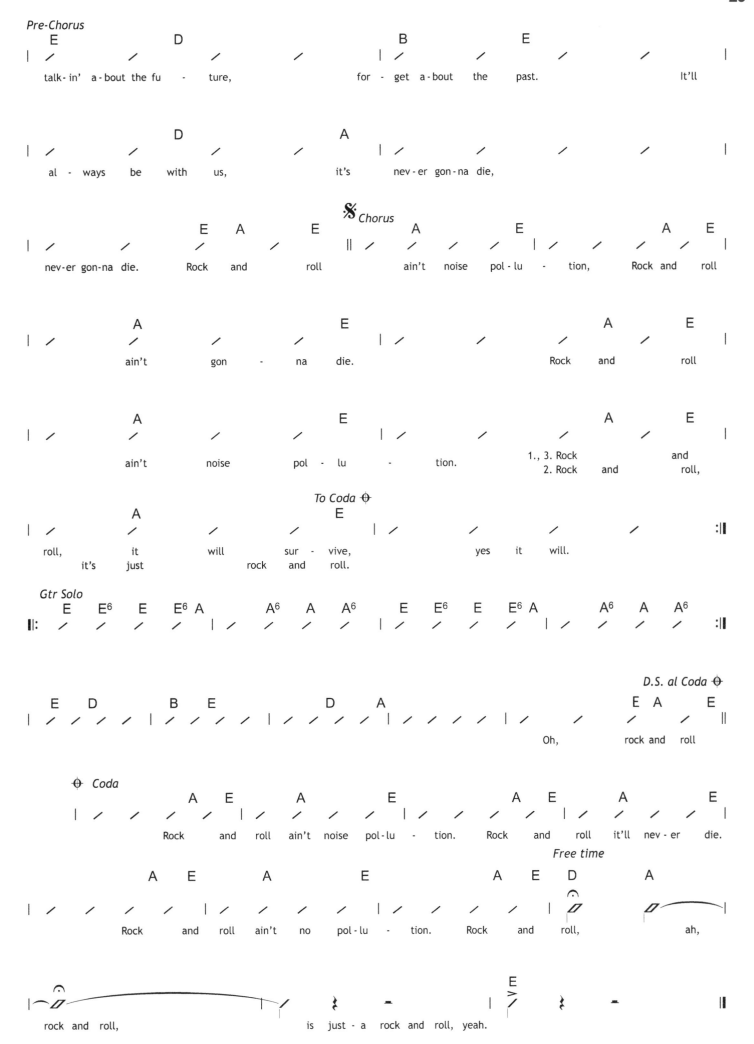

SHOOT TO THRILL

By Angus Young and Malcolm Young and Brian Johnson

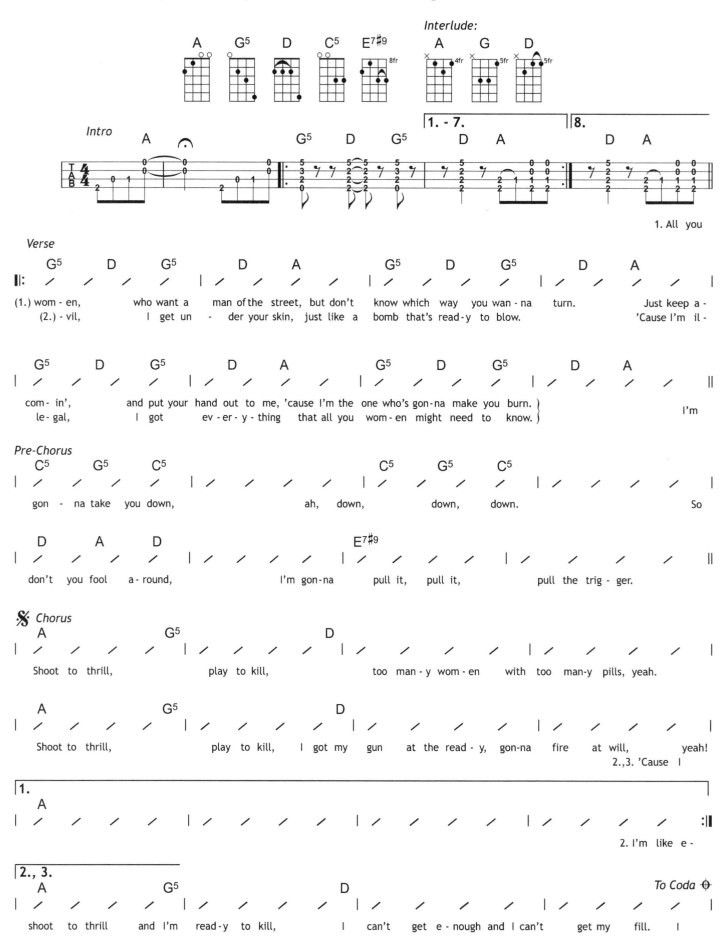

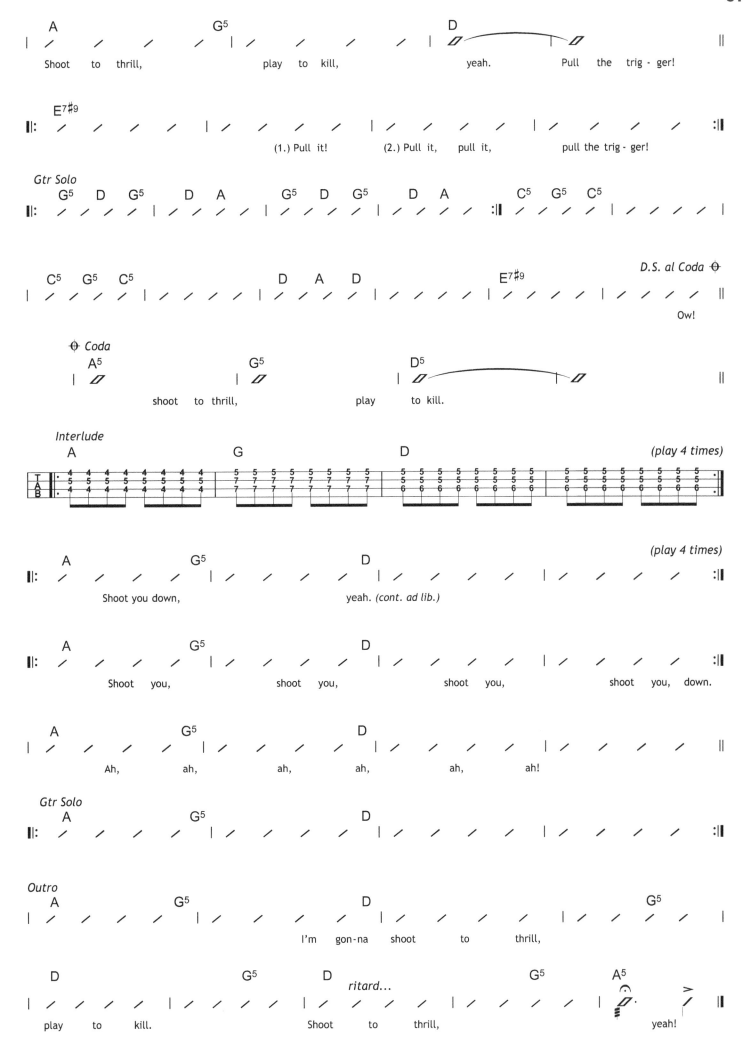

SHOT DOWN IN FLAMES

By Angus Young, Malcolm Young and Bon Scott

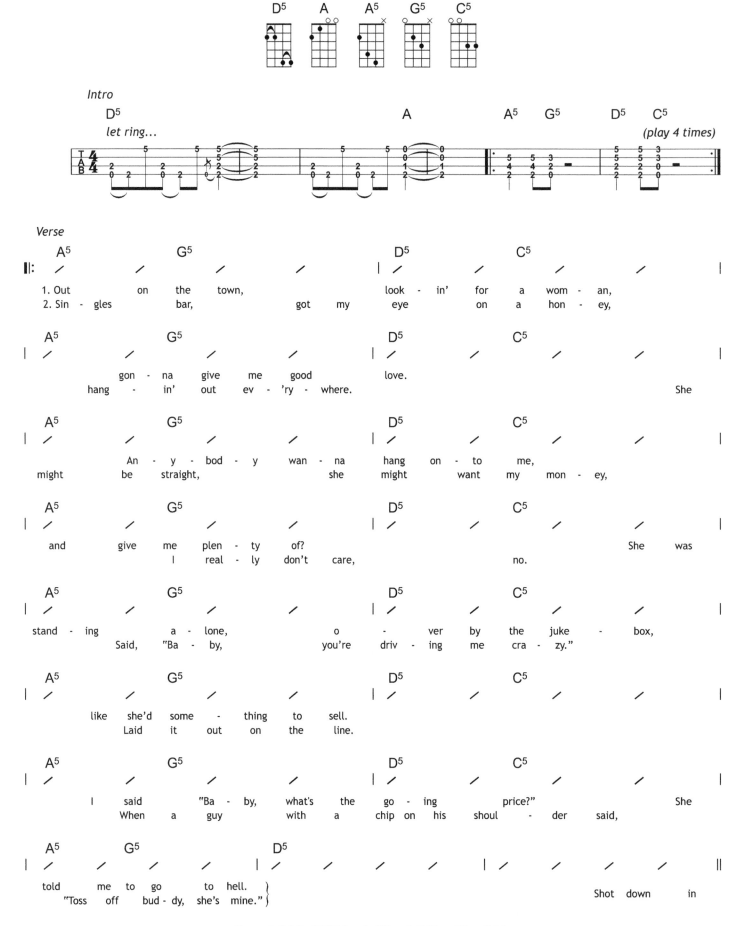

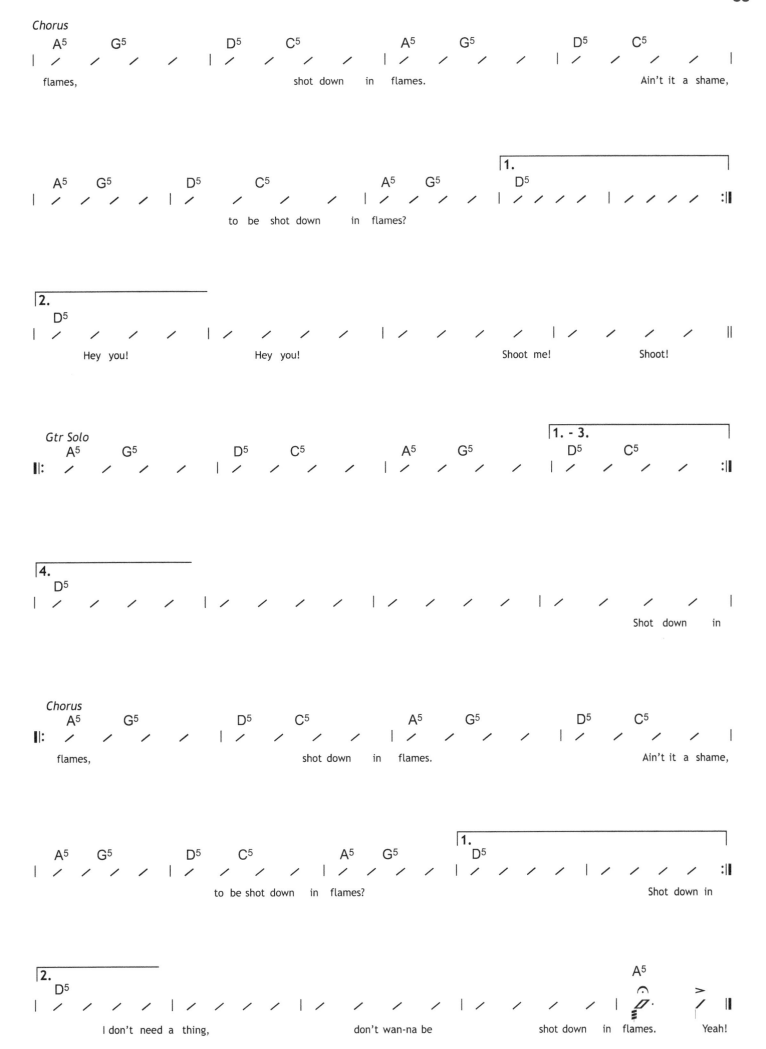

SIN CITY

By Angus Young, Malcolm Young and Bon Scott

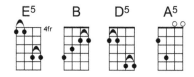

T.N.T.

By Angus Young, Malcolm Young and Bon Scott

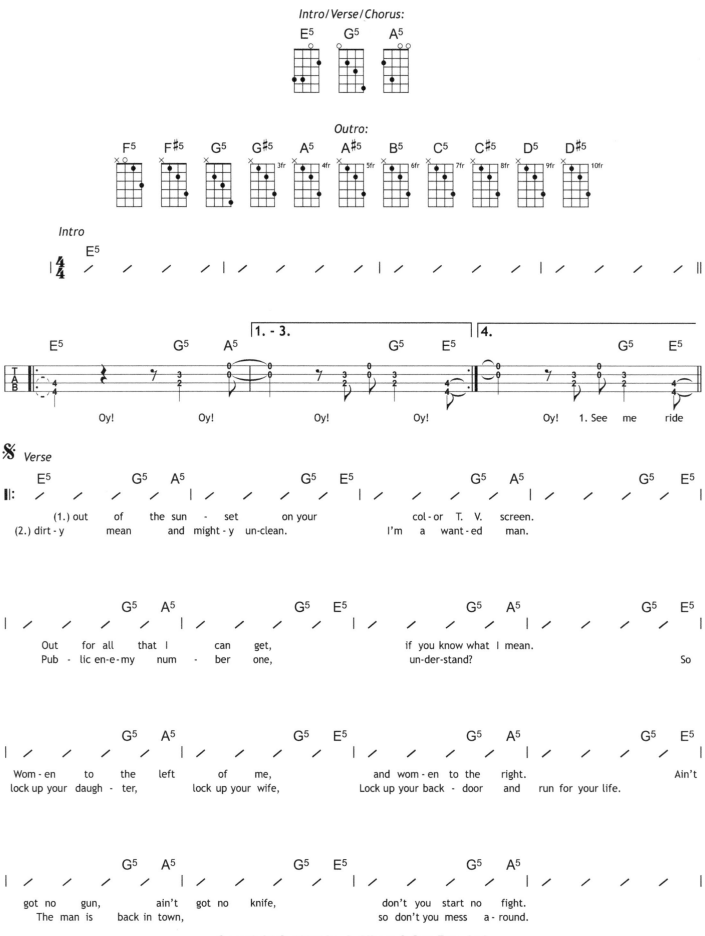

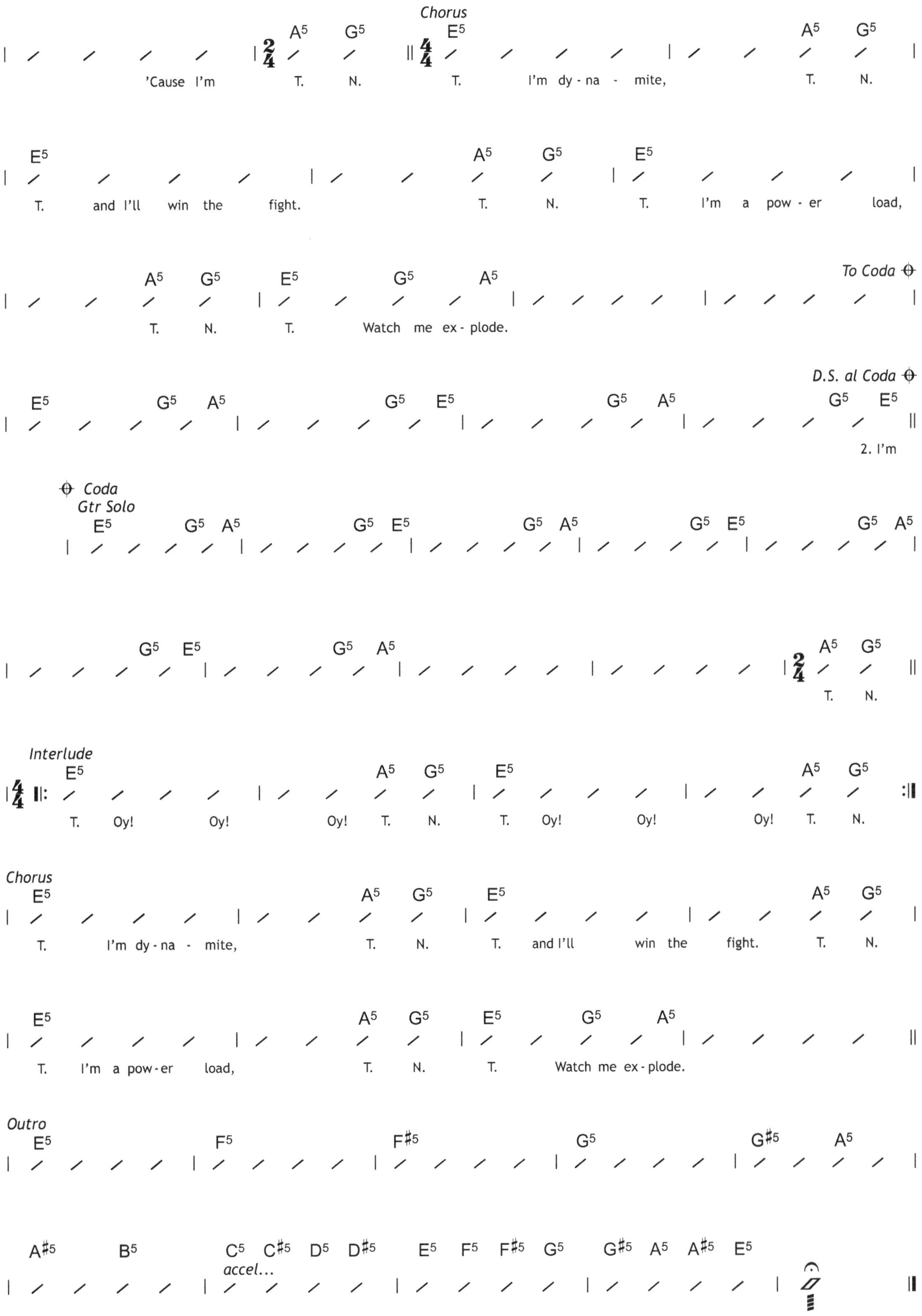
Chorus
A5 G5 E5 A5 G5
'Cause I'm T. N. T. I'm dy - na - mite, T. N.
E5 A5 G5 E5
T. and I'll win the fight. T. N. T. I'm a pow - er load,
A5 G5 E5 G5 A5
T. N. T. Watch me ex - plode.
To Coda
E5 G5 A5 G5 E5 G5 A5 G5 E5
D.S. al Coda
2. I'm
Coda
Gtr Solo
E5 G5 A5 G5 E5 G5 A5 G5 E5 G5 A5
G5 E5 G5 A5 A5 G5
T. N.
Interlude
E5 A5 G5 E5 A5 G5
T. Oy! Oy! Oy! T. N. T. Oy! Oy! Oy! T. N.
Chorus
E5 A5 G5 E5 A5 G5
T. I'm dy - na - mite, T. N. T. and I'll win the fight. T. N.
E5 A5 G5 E5 G5 A5
T. I'm a pow - er load, T. N. T. Watch me ex - plode.
Outro
E5 F5 F♯5 G5 G♯5 A5
A♯5 B5 C5 C♯5 D5 D♯5 E5 F5 F♯5 G5 G♯5 A5 A♯5 E5
accel...

WALK ALL OVER YOU

By Angus Young, Malcolm Young and Bon Scott

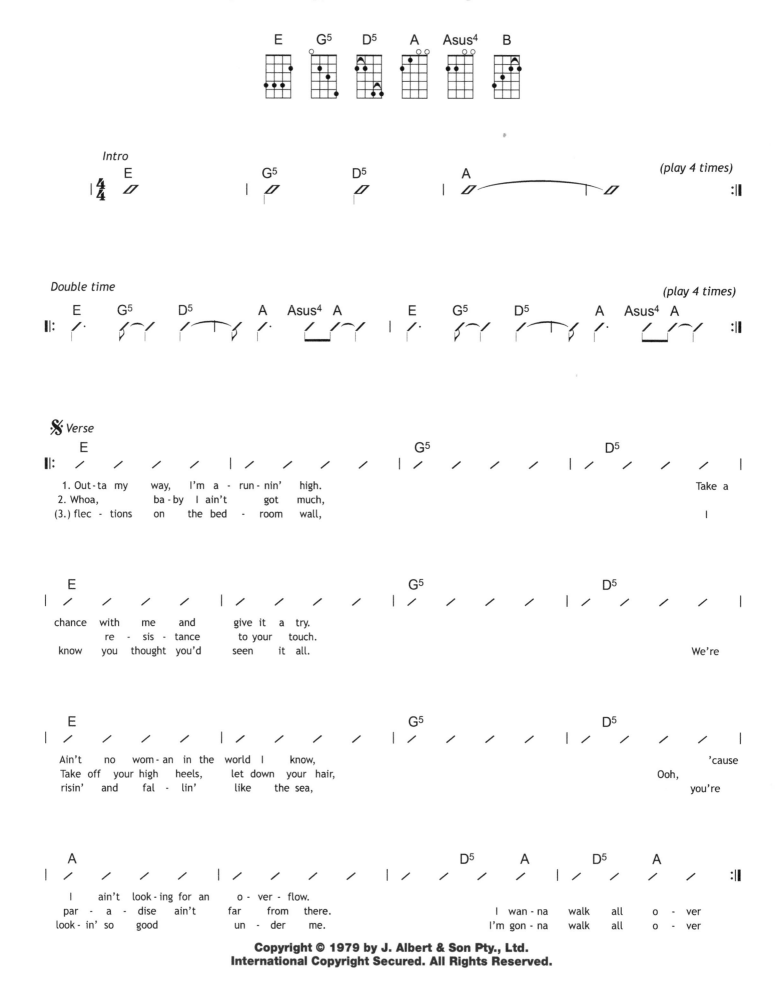

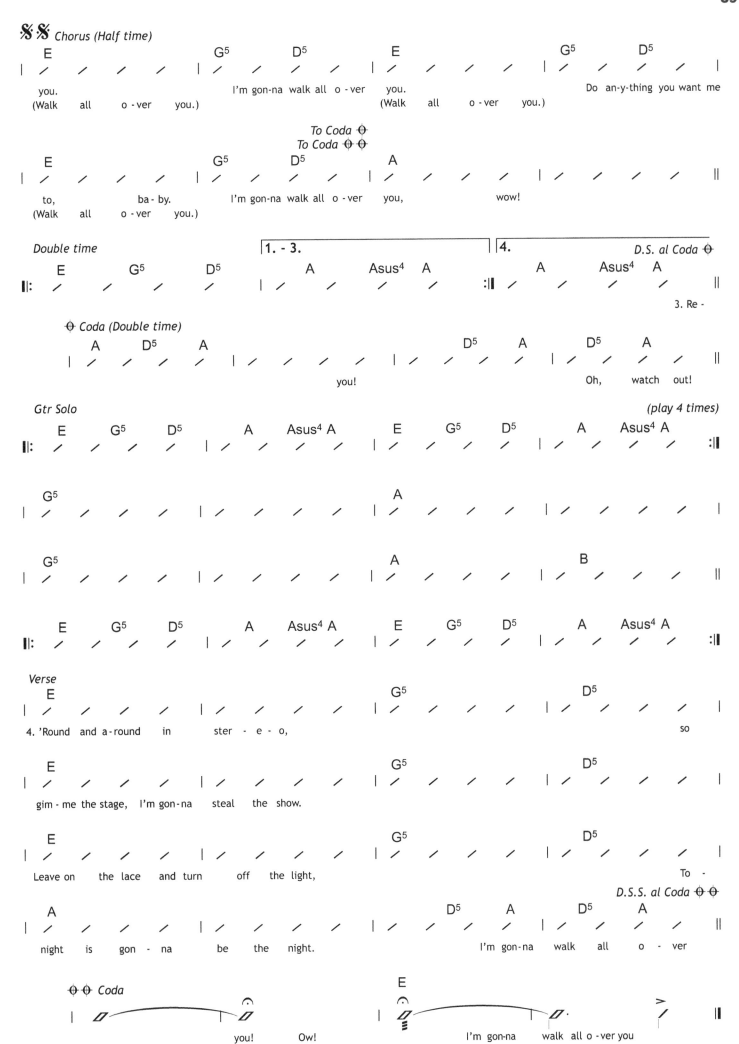

WHAT DO YOU DO FOR MONEY HONEY

By Angus Young, Malcolm Young and Brian Johnson

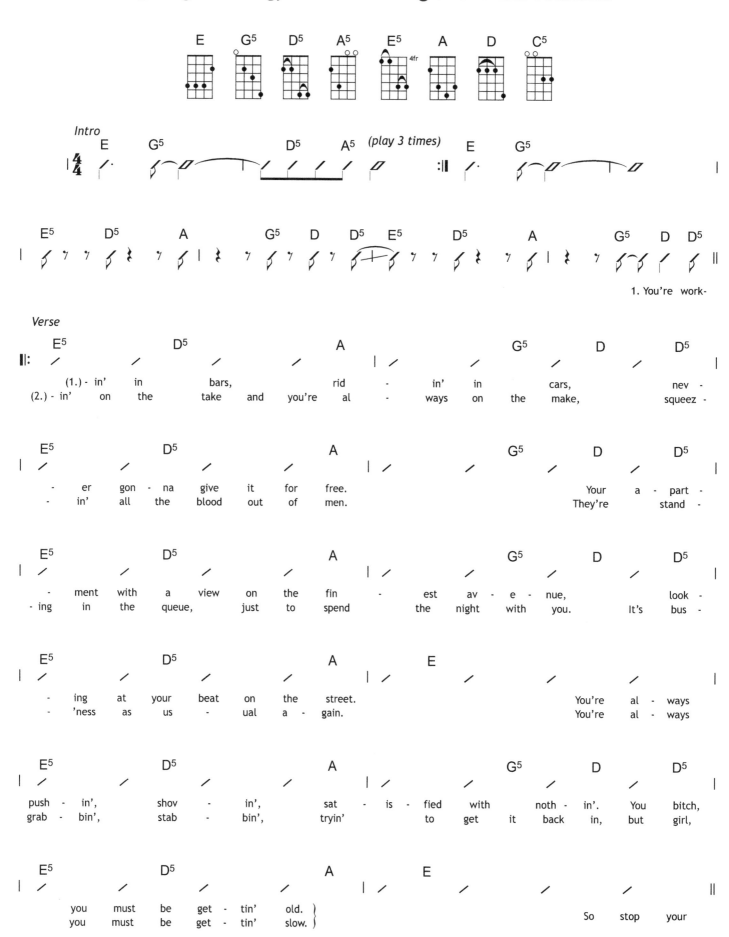

Pre-Chorus

E5   D5   A   G5   D   D5

love   on   the   road,   all   your   dig - gin'   for   gold.   You   make   me

E5   D5   A5

won - der,   yes   I   won - der,   I   won - der.

Chorus

E   G5   D5   A5   E   G5   D5   A5

Hon - ey,   what do ya do for   mon - ey?

E   G5   D5   A5   E   G5   D5   A5

Hon - ey,   what do ya do for   mon - ey?

1.

E5   D5   A   G5   D   D5   E5   D5   A   G5   D   D5

2. You're lov-

2.

E5

What do   you   do   for   mon-ey,   hon-ey,   how   d'ya   get   your   kicks?

What do   you   do   for   mon-ey,   hon-ey,   how   d'ya   get   your   licks?   Go!

Gtr Solo   (play 4 times)

A5 C5   D5   C5 A5   C5   D5   C5 A5   E5   G5   D   D5

(play 3 times)

E5   D5   A   G5   D   D5   E5   D5   A5

Chorus   (play 3 times)

E   G5   D5   A5   E   G5   D5   A5

Hon - ey,   what do ya do for   mon - ey?

E   G5   D5   A5   E   G5

Hon - ey,   what do ya do for   mon - ey?   What you

ritard...   D5   A5   E

gon-na do?   Ah,   what you gon-na do?

WHO MADE WHO

By Angus Young and Malcolm Young and Brian Johnson

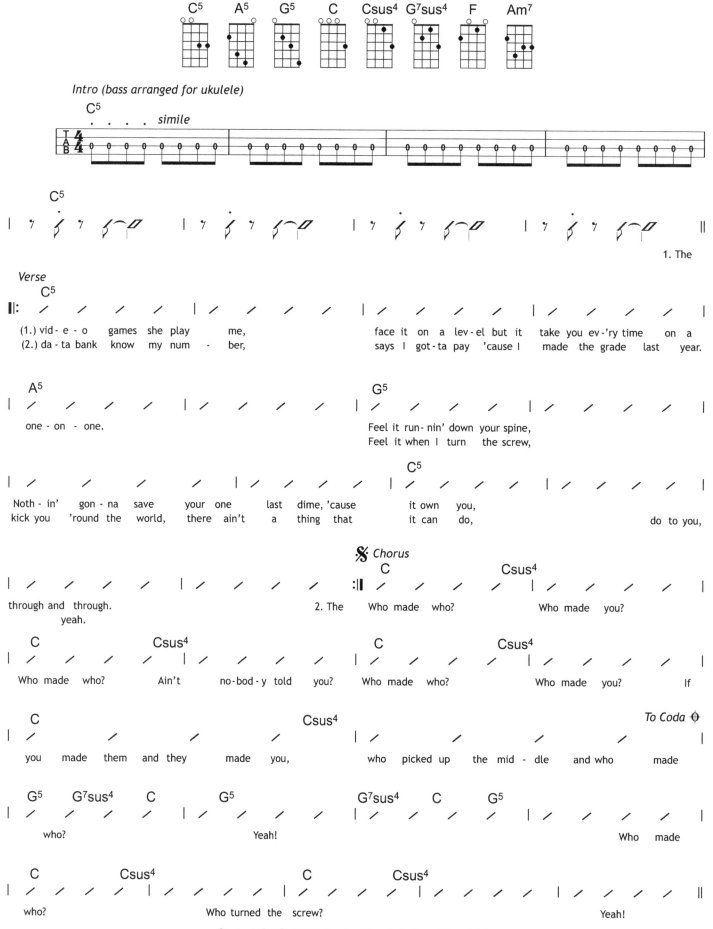

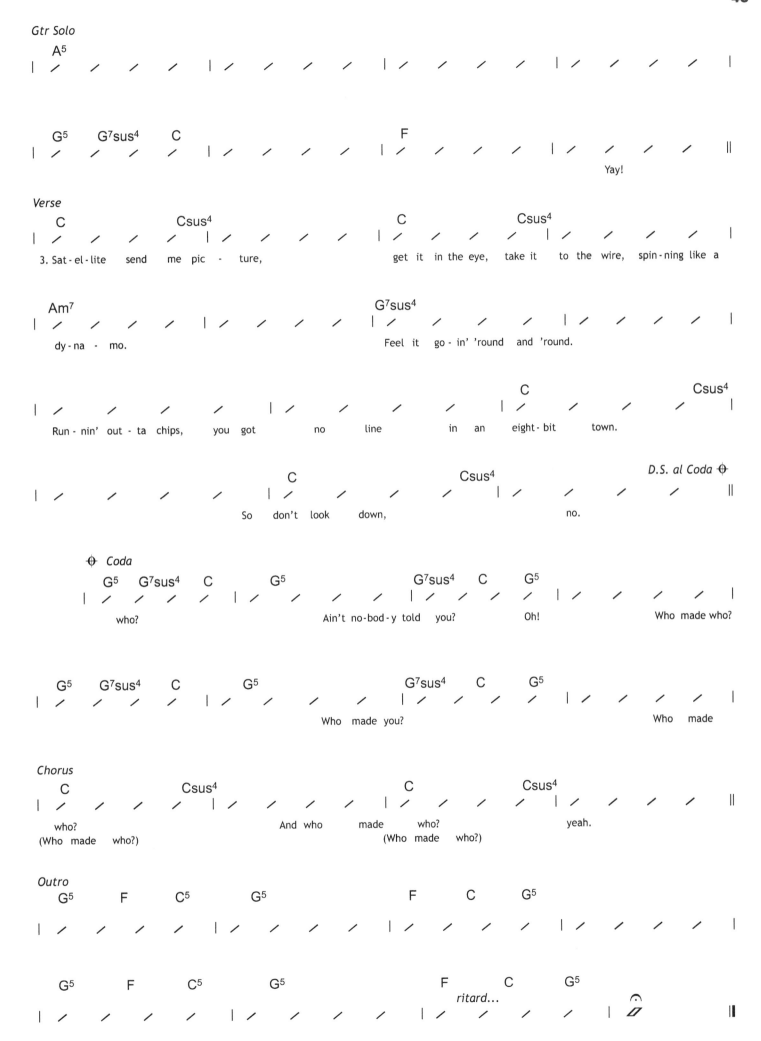

WHOLE LOTTA ROSIE

By Ronald Scott, Angus Young and Malcolm Young

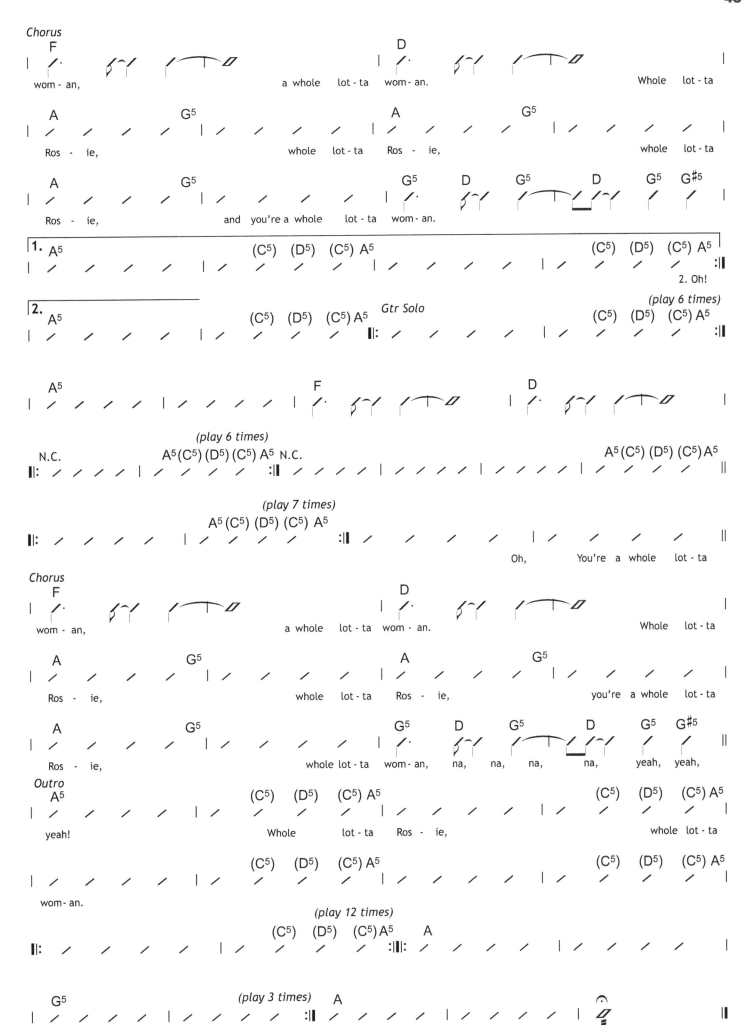

YOU SHOOK ME ALL NIGHT LONG
By Angus Young, Malcolm Young and Brian Johnson

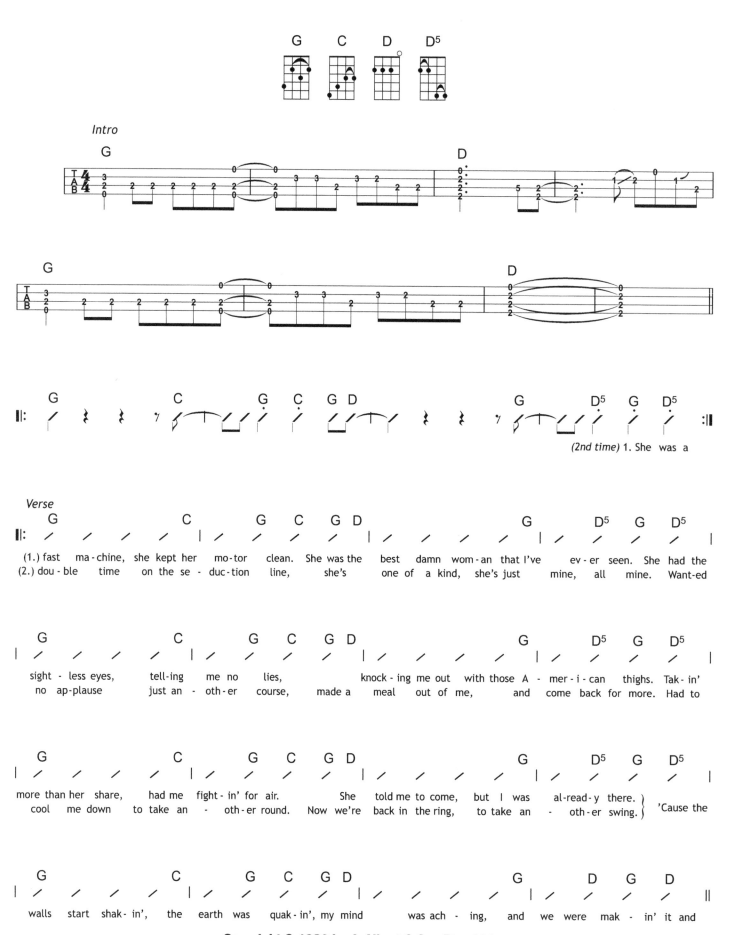

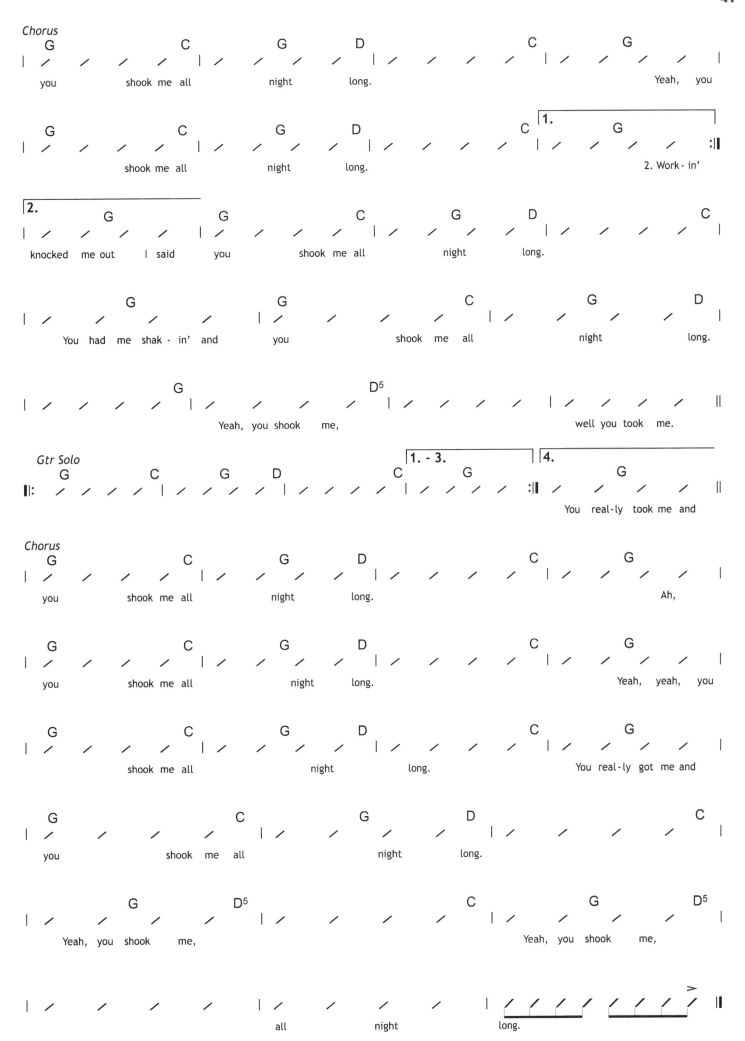

UKULELE CHORD CHART

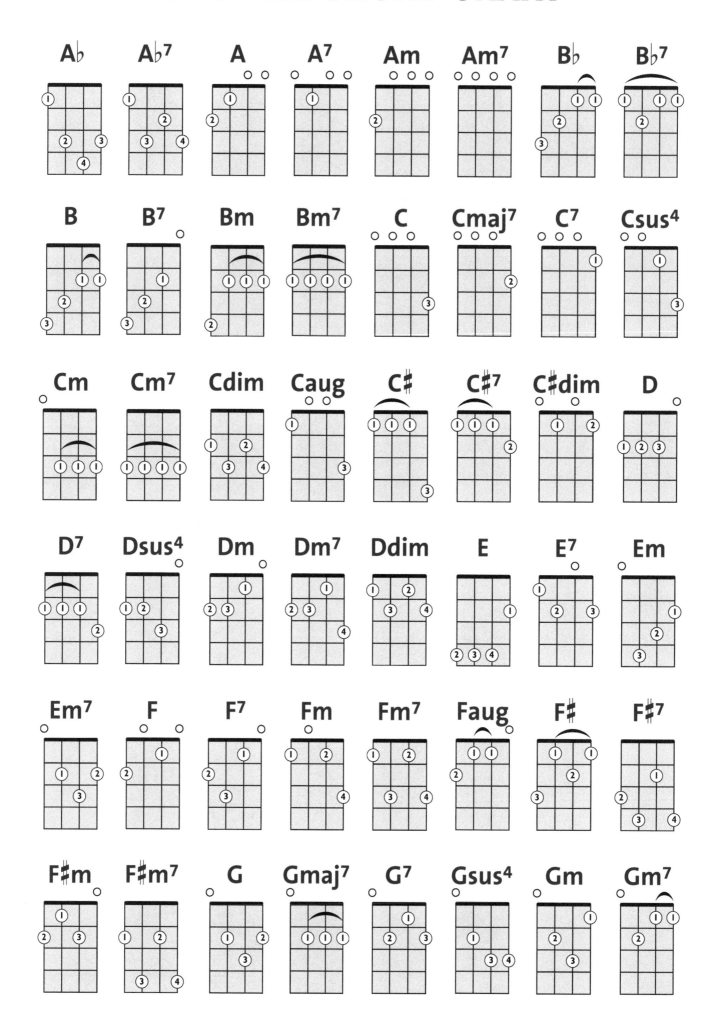